BY KATHRYN WALTON

VISIT AMERICA'S NATIONAL PARKS!

VISIT YELLOWSTONE NATIONAL PARK!

Enslow PUBLISHING

Please visit our website, www.enslow.com. For a free color catalog of all our high-quality books, call toll free 1-800-398-2504 or fax 1-877-980-4454.

Library of Congress Cataloging-in-Publication Data
Names: Walton, Kathryn, 1993- author.
Title: Visit Yellowstone National Park! / Kathryn Walton.
Description: Buffalo, NY : Enslow Publishing, [2025] | Series: Visit America's national parks! | Includes index.
Identifiers: LCCN 2024008151 | ISBN 9781978540668 (library binding) | ISBN 9781978540651 (paperback) | ISBN 9781978540675 (ebook)
Subjects: LCSH: Yellowstone National Park–Juvenile literature.
Classification: LCC F722 .W358 2025 | DDC 978.7/52–dc23/eng/20240220
LC record available at https://lccn.loc.gov/2024008151

Published in 2025 by
Enslow Publishing
2544 Clinton Street
Buffalo, NY 14224

Portions of this work were originally authored by Frances Nagle and published as *Yellowstone National Park*. All new material in this edition is authored by Kathryn Walton.

Designer: Tanya Dellaccio Keeney
Editor: Natalie Humphrey

Photo credits: Series Art (illustration) khezy licious/Shutterstock.com; cover (photo) Lorcel/Shutterstock.com; p 5 Rainer Lesniewski/Shutterstock.com; p. 7 (top) Courtesty of Library of Congress; p. 7 (bottom) Prachaya Roekdeethaweesab/Shutterstock.com; p. 9 Kate Scott/Shutterstock.com; p. 11 Kateryna Zhezlo/Shutterstock.com; p. 13 Max Studio/Shutterstock.com; p. 15 (top) Janson George/Shutterstock.com; p. 15 (bottom) Dancestrokes/Shutterstock.com; p. 17 YegoroV/Shutterstock.com; p. 19 (top) Tim Stirling/Shutterstock.com; p. 19 (bottom) Frank Fischbach/Shutterstock.com.

Some of the images in this book illustrate individuals who are models. The depictions do not imply actual situations or events.

Printed in the United States of America

CPSIA compliance information: Batch #CSENS25: For further information contact Enslow Publishing at 1-800-398-2504.

CONTENTS

Words in the glossary appear in **bold** type the first time they are used in the text.

WELCOME TO YELLOWSTONE

What's the oldest national park in the United States? Yellowstone National Park! Yellowstone's beautiful **landscape** has been kept safe since March 1, 1872. Today, the park is visited by millions of people every year. Those looking for adventure can hike on the many trails. There are also many places to camp in Yellowstone.

Even if hiking and camping aren't for you, many people enjoy the water features in the park. You can also spot wild animals in Yellowstone!

Yellowstone National Park is mostly found in northwestern Wyoming, but some parts are in Montana and Idaho.

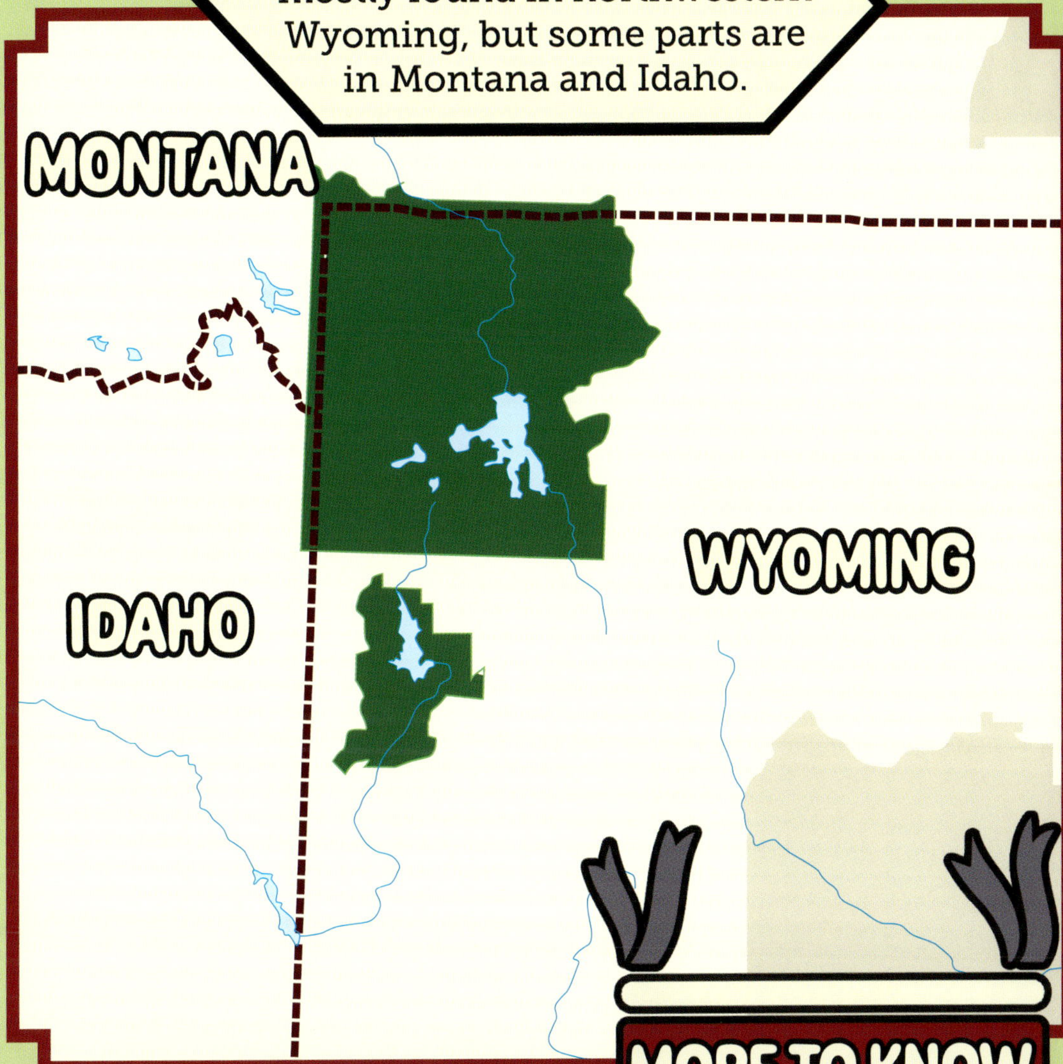

YELLOWSTONE NATIONAL PARK

MORE TO KNOW

Yellowstone is one of the oldest national parks in the world!

THE FIRST PEOPLE IN YELLOWSTONE

Archaeologists believe people have lived in the Yellowstone area for 13,000 to 14,000 years. Around 1400 CE, one group of Native Americans called the Tukudika began living there. The Tukudika are part of the Shoshone people.

It wasn't until 1807 that white **explorers** came to Yellowstone. Soon, fur trappers and others interested in the **topography** and special water features made their way to Yellowstone.

MAP OF YELLOWSTONE, 1881

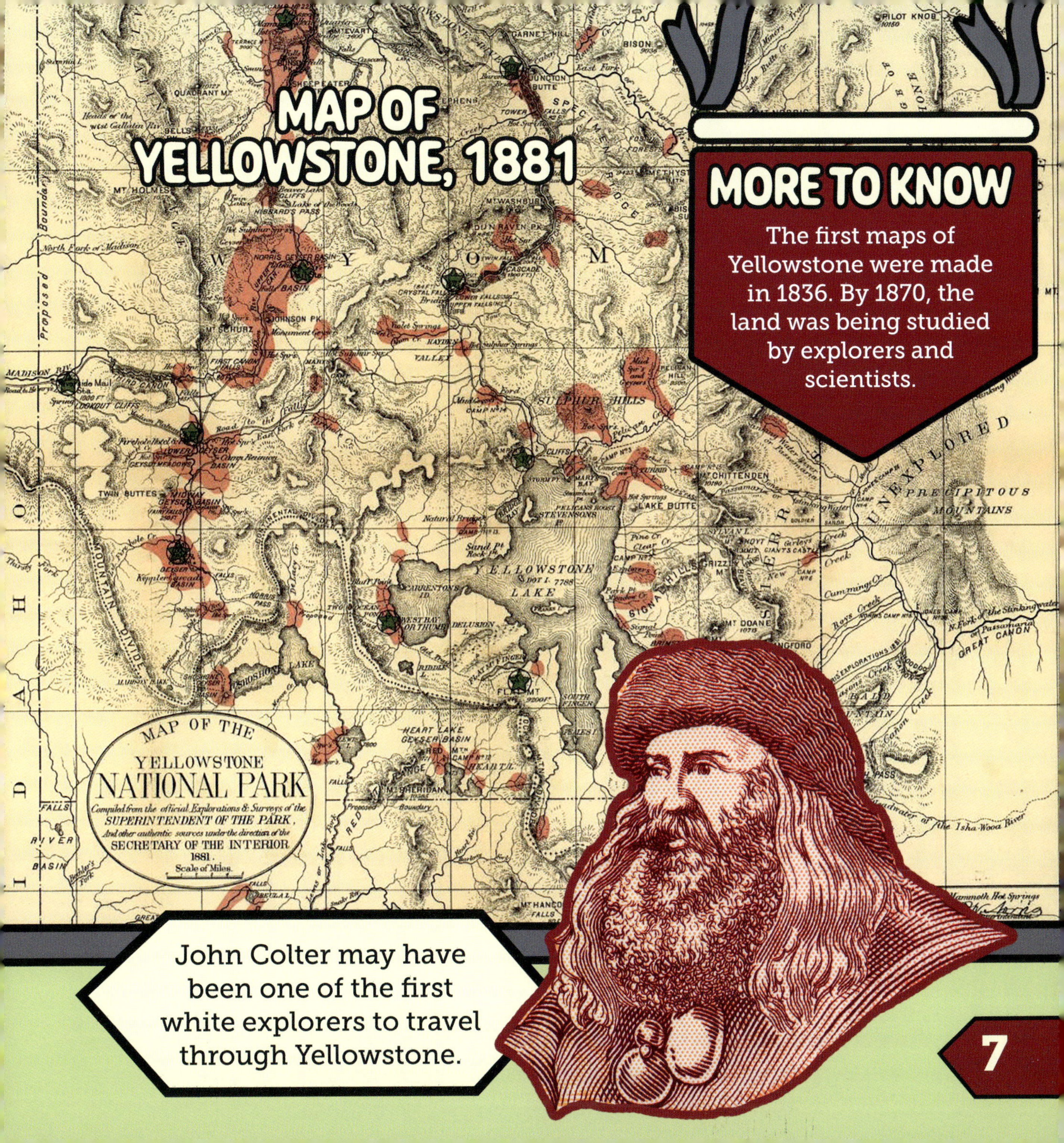

MORE TO KNOW

The first maps of Yellowstone were made in 1836. By 1870, the land was being studied by explorers and scientists.

John Colter may have been one of the first white explorers to travel through Yellowstone.

BECOMING A NATIONAL PARK

During the 1860s, people became worried about the natural landscape of the United States. They began asking the U.S. government to **protect** many beautiful and important natural areas in the country. In 1872, Yellowstone was the first of these areas to become a national park.

It wasn't enough, however. Hunters were killing too many animals, and visitors weren't taking care of the park. In 1886, the park was put under the care of the U.S. Army.

FORT YELLOWSTONE

The U.S. Army protected the animals and land from poachers, or people who illegally hunt animals for their meat and fur.

MORE TO KNOW

The U.S. Army soldiers **patrolled** the park. In 1910, 324 soldiers were stationed at Fort Yellowstone in Yellowstone National Park.

VOLCANOES!

About 2 million years ago, a volcano that had been forming for a long time in the Yellowstone area **erupted**. A volcano is an opening in Earth's crust through which **magma** sometimes flows. It erupted again about 700,000 years later and two more times after that. These events left behind a caldera, or a huge, bowl-shaped landform.

Today, the Yellowstone volcano is still active. Scientists watch the volcano carefully but don't believe it will erupt anytime soon.

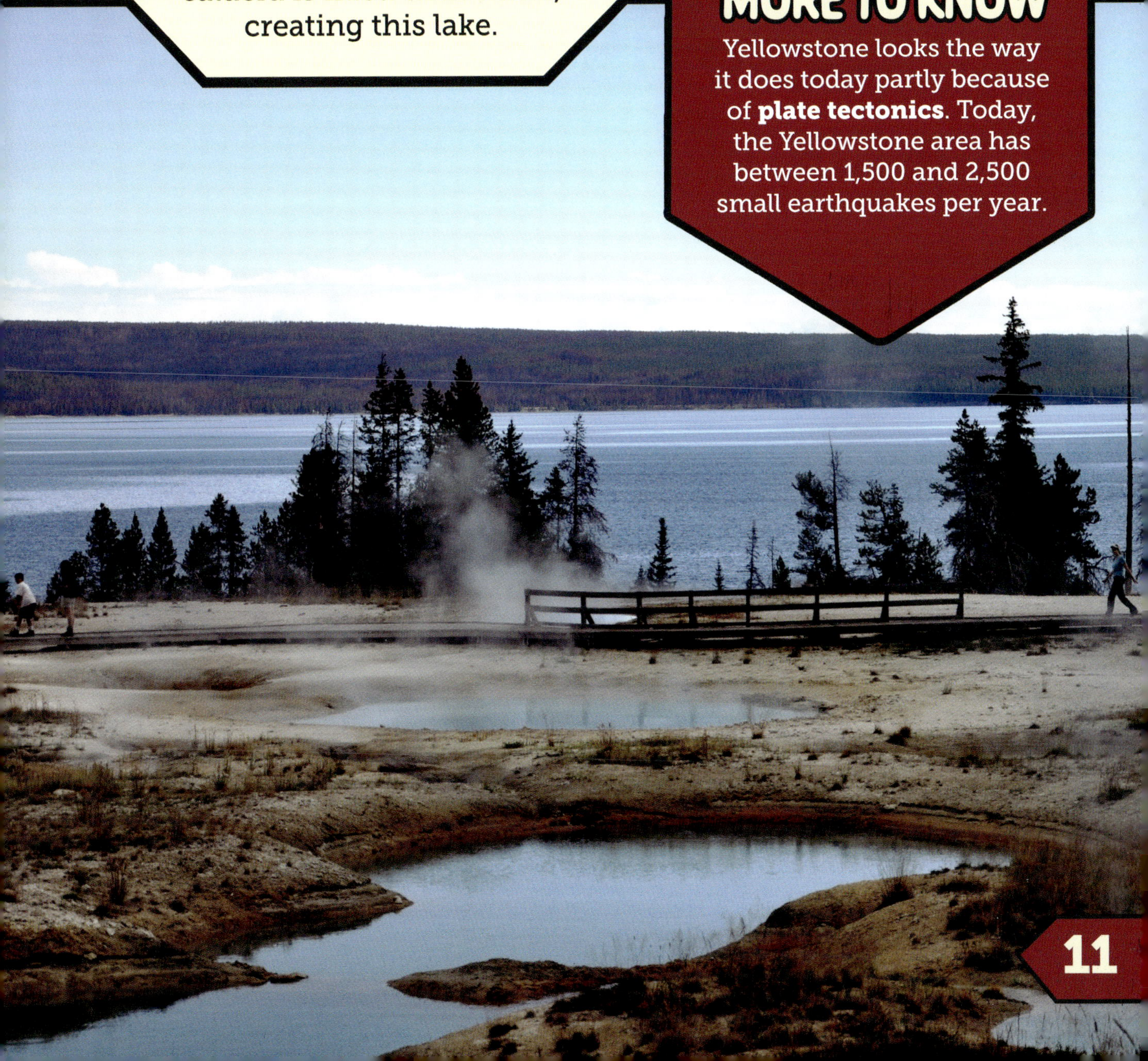

Much of the Yellowstone caldera is filled with water, creating this lake.

MORE TO KNOW

Yellowstone looks the way it does today partly because of **plate tectonics**. Today, the Yellowstone area has between 1,500 and 2,500 small earthquakes per year.

THE GRAND CANYON OF THE YELLOWSTONE

The Yellowstone River created a lot of features in the park. The river wore away rock in one area to create a canyon that's 20 miles (32 km) long. This canyon is called the Grand Canyon of the Yellowstone.

The river also forms the Upper and Lower Falls of Yellowstone. At 308 feet (94 m) high, the Lower Falls are taller than Niagara Falls by about 120 feet (37 m)! Hikers looking for adventure can hike to the top of the falls.

MORE TO KNOW

Scientists believe the Grand Canyon of the Yellowstone may have first formed between 140,000 to 160,000 years ago.

The Lower Falls is one of the most photographed places in Yellowstone National Park.

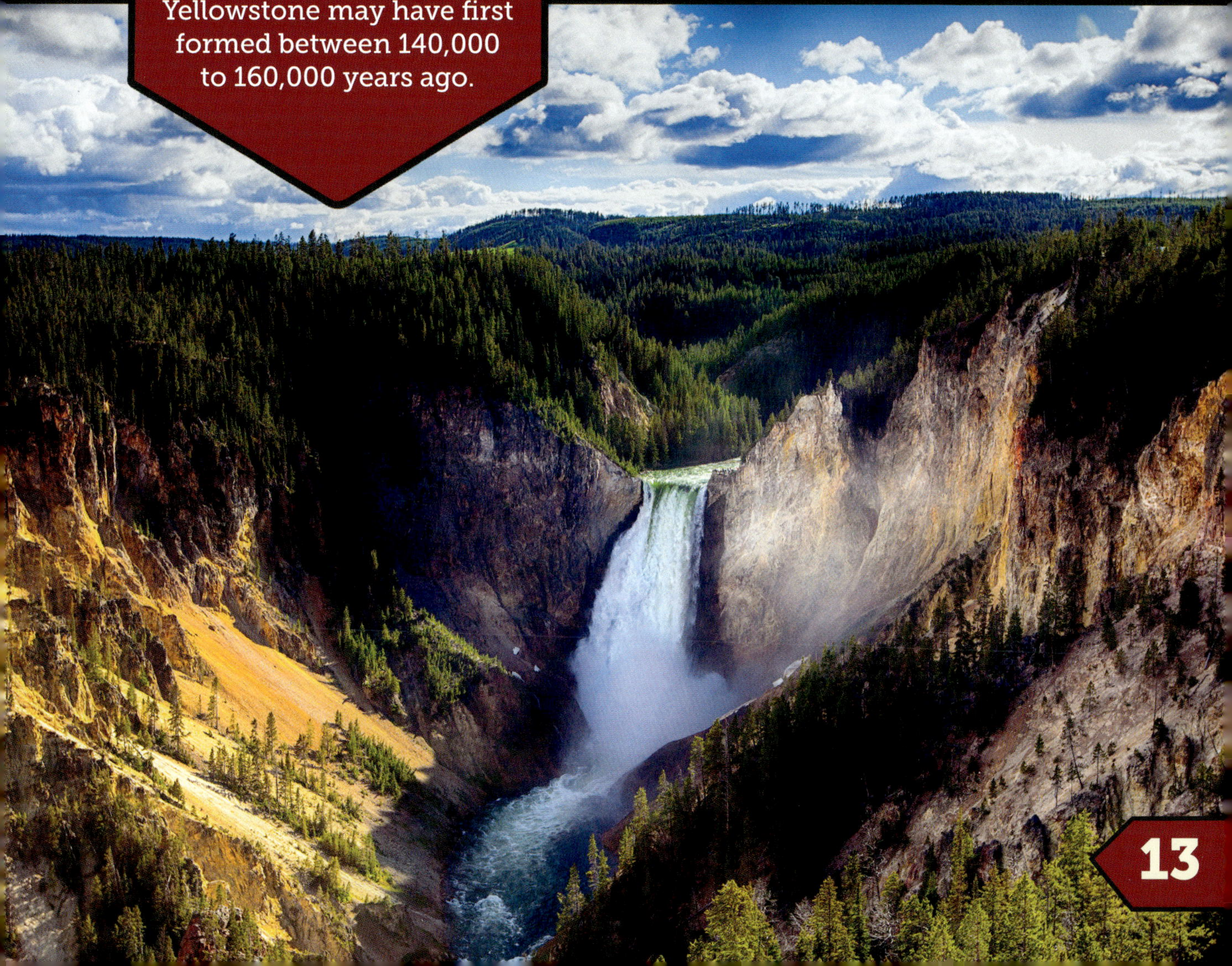

GEYSERS

One of the most well-known sites in Yellowstone National Park is a **geyser** called Old Faithful. It's in the Upper Geyser Basin west of the center of the park. It "faithfully" erupts about every 90 minutes, earning its name by staying on time.

There are about 300 other geysers in Yellowstone. In fact, visitors can find about 10,000 **hydrothermal** features throughout the park. There's even a hot spring you can visit!

Around two-thirds of the geysers in the world are in Yellowstone National Park.

MORE TO KNOW

All the hydrothermal features in the park are caused by magma heating water underground.

YELLOWSTONE WILDLIFE

Most of Yellowstone is covered in thick forest. Most of the trees are lodgepole pines.

The forests provide a great home for animals such as foxes, elk, and mule deer. Songbirds and woodpeckers are the most common birds in the park. More than 300 kinds of birds live there for at least part of the year. Beavers live in and along the many lakes and streams in the park. You can also find trout and other fish in these waters.

MORE TO KNOW

The National Park Service advises giving animals such as bison and elk at least 25 yards (23 m) of space, or two buses worth. Animals such as bears and wolves should be given a lot more space, at least 100 yards (91 m)!

Between 3,000 to 6,000 bison live in Yellowstone National Park.

PETRIFIED WOOD

Have you ever heard of a petrified tree? "Petrified" means "turned to stone." A tree can become petrified over a long period of time as **minerals** replace the tree's wood. Yellowstone National Park has the greatest number of petrified trees in the world!

You can find many of these petrified trees at Specimen Ridge. However, one of these trees stands alone in the northeast part of the park. Simply called the Petrified Tree, this tree was once a redwood in a forest of other redwoods.

It's illegal to take any pieces of petrified wood you find in Yellowstone.

MORE TO KNOW

A volcanic eruption killed the other redwood trees around the Petrified Tree.

THE PETRIFIED TREE

PLANNING YOUR VISIT

Yellowstone National Park is open year-round. Many people hike or camp in the forests and explore the many special features found in the park. While you can visit anytime, many people visit during June, July, and August. The best time to visit to avoid crowds is during April, September, and October. During some seasons, though, some parts of the park are closed.

No matter what time you visit, Yellowstone National Park is a place you must see!

MORE TO KNOW

Make sure to check the weather before heading to Yellowstone. The summers can be hot, but the park is cold enough for snow during the winter.

YELLOWSTONE NATIONAL PARK

THE FACTS

ESTABLISHED

1872

SIZE

3,472 square miles (8,992 sq km)

NUMBER OF VISITORS EACH YEAR

around 3 million

NATIVE WILDLIFE

black bears, coyotes, wolves, woodpeckers, elk, and more

NATIVE PLANTS

Douglas firs, wildflowers, lodgepole pines, and more

MUST-SEE STOPS

Old Faithful, Specimen Ridge, the Grand Canyon of the Yellowstone

GLOSSARY

archaeologist: Someone who studies the tools and other objects left behind by ancient people.

erupt: To burst forth.

explorer: A person that searches to find out new things.

geyser: A spring that shoots heated water and steam from a crack in Earth.

hydrothermal: Having to do with hot water, especially mixed with minerals from cooling.

landscape: All of the features in an area of land that can be seen.

magma: Hot, liquid rock inside Earth.

mineral: Matter in the ground that forms rocks.

patrol: The act of going from one place to another in a set area to make sure no crimes are being committed.

plate tectonics: The study of the movement of the plates, or large pieces of rock, that form Earth's surface.

protect: To keep safe.

topography: The natural and human-made features of a place.

FOR YOUR INFORMATION

Books

Frisch, Nate. *Yellowstone National Park*. Mankato, MN: Creative Education and Creative Paperbacks, 2025.

Tomlinson, Marla. *Yellowstone National Park: A Natural Wonder*. Chicago, IL: Norwood House Press, 2024.

Websites

National Geographic Kids: Yellowstone National Park
kids.nationalgeographic.com/nature/article/yellowstone
Learn more about the history of Yellowstone National Park and what you can find there.

National Park Service: Yellowstone
www.nps.gov/yell/learn/kidsyouth/index.htm
Find out more things you can do on your visit to Yellowstone National Park.

INDEX